Where We Lay Down

Where We Lay Down

Poems by

Jeffrey Franklin

Cover design by Shay Culligan

ISBN: 978-1-954353-95-4

Kelsay Books
502 South 1040 East, A-119
American Fork, Utah 84003
Kelsaybooks.com

In memory of
Margaret Trotter Lane (1931–2017)
and for Henry Trotter Franklin

Acknowledgments

I am grateful to the following journals, in which versions of these poems appeared, and to their editors, whose decisions have supported my poetry:

Arkansas Review: "Huck Finn at Forty-One"
Cimarron Review: "Lawrence from New Mexico, 27 October, 1922"
Common Ground Review: "Julian Bream"
Cumberland Poetry Review: "Dun Aengus"
Cutthroat: "War Porno"
Diner: "My Self My Other"
Dogwood: "Apologia to the Opossums" section IV (as "Apologia to the Opossums (IV)")
Hudson Review: "In Search of the Lost Indian Princess" (as "Florida"), "Porc d'Espine"
Icarus: "The Otter and the Shark"
Iron Horse: "McGaulie's Polo Grounds"
Many Mountains Moving: "Awake"
Measure: "Apologia to the Opossums" sections I and II, "How Far We Never Get Beyond Our Dreams"
New England Review: "To a Student Who Reads 'The Second Coming' as Sexual Autobiography"
North Carolina Literary Review: "Squirrelly," "The Walls of the West of Ireland"
Quadrant: "The Road to Canberra, and Beyond"
Rattle: "The Excitement of Getting a Room with a Minibar" (from "Germanic Traincar Constructions"), "Living Right"
River Oak Review: "The Leggers"
Shenandoah: "Commerce & Gender in the New South"
Southern Poetry Review: "Autumnal Equinox," "Dungeness," "Sky"
storySouth: "Kosciusko, Mississippi," "Where We Lay Down"

"The City That Chooses You" and "The Otter and the Shark" were part of a manuscript that received the 2001 Robert H. Winner Memorial Award from The Poetry Society of America. Thanks to the Society, the Winner family, and Stephanie Strickland.

"To a Student Who Reads 'The Second Coming' as Sexual Autobiography" appeared in *Best American Poetry 2002,* thanks to C. Dale Young and the late Robert Creeley.

"Julian Bream" was anthologized in *How to Be this Man: The Walter Pavlich Memorial Poetry Anthology* from Swan Scythe Press (2003), thanks to Sandra McPherson.

With gratitude to William Logan, who indeed winnows and hones.

I bow to James Applewhite, Sidney Wade, Catherine Carter, and James Najarian, poetry mentors and friends who generously gave me their time, support, and good spirits. Thanks also to Randall Mann.

Thanks to my colleagues Brian Barker, who lent a masterly hand in reshaping this manuscript, and Wayne Miller, who gently tutored me in aspects of acting as a professional poet.

For his photographic and design skills, thanks to nephew Maximilian Badham, founder of Informal clothing who sports a beautiful self-designed tattoo of Max from *Where the Wild Things Are.*

Thanks to Meril Shane, Mad Meril Photography, for the author photos on this book and at www.jeffreyfranklin.com.

With gratitude to my father, James Rodman Franklin, for his example of being true to his art and for the seven of his artworks sampled on the cover and inside this collection. His architecture stands throughout Tennessee, and his watercolors, drawings, and etchings, which he showed and sold for over 50 years, grace homes and collections across the Southeast, in San Luis Obispo, CA, where he lived a while, and in Norway, where he gave an invited show.

Contents

Fathers and Sons

Sons and Fathers   16
How Far We Never Get Beyond Our Dreams   18
McGaulie's Polo Grounds   19
Personal Effects   21
Julian Bream   23
Sky   24

Making Love

Commerce & Gender in the New South   28
My Self My Other   30
Among the Surma of the Kormu Valley,
    A *National Geographic* Photographer   32
Queen Kong Storms the Kitchen (or, Bathing the
    Baby in the Sink)   34
To a Student Who Reads "The Second Coming"
    as Sexual Autobiography   35
The Otter and the Shark   36
Living Right   37

Making War

Huck Finn at Forty-One   42
"Honk for Peace"   46
War Porno   48
You Talkin' to Me, Pilgrim?   49
Dun Aengus   51

Homing

Awake   56
Dungeness   58
Kosciusko, Mississippi   61
Lawrence from New Mexico, 27 October, 1922   62
The City That Chooses You   63
The Road to Canberra, and Beyond   65
The Walls of the West of Ireland   66
The Persistence of Place   68

Totem Animals

Porc d'Espine   72
Further Reflections on the Death of a Porcupine   74
Mouse Poem for La Petite   76
Squirrelly   78
Chocolate and the Manatees   80
Apologia to the Opossums   82

Full Emptiness

Where We Lay Down   88
The Leggers   89
In Search of the Lost Indian Princess   90
The *Mackinaw* Heads South   92
Germanic Traincar Constructions   94
Anatman   101
Autumnal Equinox   103

Fathers and Sons

Our world is very dusty, Uncle. Let us work.
One day the sickness shall pass from the earth for good.
The orchard will bloom; someone will play the guitar.
Our work will be seen as strong and clean and good.
       And all that we suffered through having existed
       Shall be forgotten as though it had never existed.

—Donald Justice, "There is a Gold Light in Certain Old
   Paintings"

Sons and Fathers

Jimmy, the plumber, kneeling beside the PVC cleanout,
shit bespeckling his forearm, replies to my small-talk question,
"My Dad was murdered a year ago this Sunday."
My fretting over clay pipes sunk in The Depression,
invading roots, backhoe reared like Godzilla in the flowerbed,
drains away to a knock at the door, the face, the gun.

The mind swerves from one's own father, glimpses the gun
Mr. Gaye waved at Marvin, who would not shut up or get out.
How can any son get out, cribbed in the plush bed
of the coffin, voice snuffed? How could Isaac question
Abraham, whose Father boiled lightning in a cyclonic depression
above him? Well, we are told, Oedipus had his day.

What man does not have to rekill his father each day?
So how could Jimmy, preempted, robbed of his gun,
do other than baptize himself in the shit of depression,
telling and retelling the story: his dad carving out
the business, whiskey and fists, unbroachable questions
scabbed over at last to an easy distance, the work a shared bed.

Ages before factories and offices robbed the marriage bed
of men at dawn, returning them in the dark, a boy's day
was his father's. Silence, mostly, the boy doing without question
what the man did, learning to string the bow, clean the gun,
sail the plow, let the saw do the work, muck out
the stalls. Then the Industrial Revolution minted depression,

along with divorce, child labor, and debtor's prison.
My mother's mother banned my father from the bed
of my birth—"This is woman's business, men keep out"—

16

and he did, into the arms of the twelve-hour workday.
Now that New Age dads trade the office and the gun
for pacifier and diaper, time-outs and all questions

painstakingly answered, what will be the son's quest?
Dad-as-friend nurtures postmodern depression,
no doubt, Freud obsolete at long last, the new Bedlam
a malaise of standardized tests and numberless guns
simulating rebellion, each new purchase a holiday
from archaic dreads. Come, Father, let us step out

into the old dark forest. No questions, no melodramatic beds
breeding depression. I know, you can rise from the dead any day,
wreathed in brimstone, finger a gun pointing the way out.

How Far We Never Get Beyond Our Dreams

I dreamt you took me down to your new office,
the elevator jolting on its cables,
the tall, dim hall through which your nameplate's brass
shown from the door. You were the sleek new boss,
just split from your father's firm. The boss's son,
I was the darling of the secretary
and toyed with inheriting the crown,
but ammonia from the blueprints made me giddy. . . .

Before I knew, I held your severed head
and cast it into a drawer like a pizza oven.
The look you gave me then, so full of sad
and knowing pity, nearly caved me in,
but the secretary closed me in her sights,
and now I have your work to do tonight.

McGaulie's Polo Grounds

There was a grey plank barn submerged in amber
where we fought duels among the tack room's shadows.
Shelved by the magazine of mallets and spurs,
tins painted with a thoroughbred's Derby pose
laced the smells of hay and urine with camphor.
Mud daubers spit-and-pasted Quonset chateaus
where swallows dipped through summer's furnace door,
and the dirt floor quaked when in a heated chukka
the ponies charged the barn-end goal like thunder.

The loft was stacked with bales up to the eaves,
and where their stagger left slim corridors
we tunneled courses deep on our hands and knees,
a sudden rat as good as a Minotaur.
Astride the fence, we tracked our fathers' jerseys,
beneath the stands eavesdropped on chatting mothers,
loosened to high cackles by daiquiris.
The wheeling mounts, the whip of mallets, the blur
and weave of scrimmage made an elegant war.

But we slipped off before the final pistol
to wade the creek that ran beside the grounds.
Roots laddered to glassy sun-streaked pools,
moss-backed rocks beneath which crawdads crowned
with jellied eyes and red antennae—cruel
claws "big as lobsters'"—reared to face us down.
Black and red feathers fanned to a paisley swirl
in one pool where a leghorn rooster drowned,
a kaleidoscopic eddy turning round.

There was an oval in the sun, the rule
of fathers rearing above us like Minotaurs.
Young men beyond their means, not long from school,
their mortgaged businesses an elegant war
for which weekend mock chivalry was cruel
reward, they swapped and then divorced the mothers.
But we slipped off before the final pistol
like whiffs of hay and urine laced with camphor
and disappeared through summer's furnace door.

Personal Effects

Each drawer and closet opened a life lived
by the ordering of the ordinary: the cuff links,
the pen nibs, the honorary medallions sorted
in engraved boxes, the bottles soldiered by the sink,
and we, with voyeur's piety, fingered all.

But there, in the back bottom drawer, mixed
with fold-worn maps and long discharged batteries,
an unpredicted cache: a jaunty sailor,
a turbaned sultan, a harlequin with "Smitty"
penned on the back—gray snaps of dead men

in their twenties, awaiting the "fancy-dress."
And you, implied behind the shutter, what
did you wear? This robe of hand-embroidered silk
from the closet's dark recesses, its wasp-legged cranes
serenely lofting the jagged snowy peaks. . . .

In the Heaven that you, if anyone, proved,
they surely pose before your camera again,
and you, who shed a tie only for fishing or bed,
preside like a shogun in this extraordinary saffron!
If we had not known you so well,

we might not have known you at all, you
in whom kindness leavened the strictest integrity
with an easy laugh, the true gentleman proved
superior by never to anyone acting superior,
smoothing the awkward into belonging.

Here, in the only heaven I know (forgive me,
Granddaddy), your peppery, sweet odor,
tinctured through decades of wear into worsteds
and tweeds, camel hair and suede, is borne
to our closets, to be filled as best we are able.

Julian Bream

Your eyes sunk deeply in chevrons of shadow,
  you played the hall as if it were the box,
and you, inside, the animus of music.
  When your hand lifted from the last of Bach's

E Minor Suite, as if to bid that chord
  safe passage, you held us for the close
to silence, pulled a crumpled hankie
  from your back pocket and wiped your nose

just as I've seen old carpenters do,
  using a rough, three-stroke motion.
I wondered then why you forsake
  your restored Baroque villa by the ocean

for a different hotel suite each evening,
  with hardly an accolade left to accrue,
sufficient wealth, your younger self
  the only performer sure to outstrip you.

For one moment I inclined to think
  of that great calling we call Art,
but then remembered another who,
  as they say of racehorses, has heart:

my stepfather, bald and stooped now too,
  puts on a suit and drives to offices
where quietness gathers 'round filed papers,
  because that's what it is he does.

Sky

I waited till dawn, then came to wake you up,
expecting you'd be burrowed in the sheets,
but when I eased the door ajar I glimpsed
you sitting up, propped on one arm, your head

inclined a little to the side, as if
the weight of dreams might pull you down again.
Then I saw your gaze had carried you out
among the shadow-nested branches.

Your age, I sat beside the road and waited,
watching rain come. I'd never seen the sky
as something wholly separate from me,
and then I did. The clouds were gray and fierce,

low against the mountain, raked by branches.
Beneath the whipping elm, I wanted them
to touch me. Just as first drops began to fall,
my father came from work and carried me in.

Until today, I've thought it was for him
I waited, he who'd come to carry me.
Gray light is sifting through the trees you know.
I close the door and leave you to the sky.

Making Love

Look out, Slim, these girls are trouble.
You dance with them they dance you back.
They talk it broad but they want it subtle
and you got too much of a mouth for that.

—Michael Donaghy, "The Bacchae"

Commerce & Gender in the New South

I. "Gentleman's Club and Exotic Car Wash"
(freeway billboard, Greensboro, NC)

The gentlemen lounge in smoking jackets and ascots
while girls come out in thongs to soap their bumpers.
Loin-clothed thugs parade leopard mascots,

and the bar is tended by Polynesian drummers.
Huge spiraling brushes lash the proffered buttocks
of girls who come out in thongs to soap the bumpers.

See-thru slickers, Wellingtons, and Gortex socks
are *de rigeur* for waitresses who serve with French polish
as huge spiraling brushes lash their proffered buttocks.

"Every make and model, Balinese to Polish,"
winks the *maitre d'*. Bondage, wax, and mudguards
are *de rigeur* for waitresses who serve with French polish.

"They'll detail your interior, for VISA or MASTERCARD,
clean you all the way down to the dipstick,"
winks the *maitre d'*. Bondage, wax, and greencards—

"exotic" for girls who share a smoke and a lipstick
before they clean you all the way down to the dipstick,
you gentlemen lounging in smoking jackets and ascots
while loin-clothed thugs parade paint-spotted mascots.

II. "Barbara's Beauty Shoppe and Chainsaw Repair"
(store-front sign, Greenville, NC)

Barbara, known as "Bob," does perms and tune-ups.
Big chrome scissors duel an art-deco chain saw
in the center of the Shoppe. Nexxus headshots and pin-ups

from Poulen logging calendars lend a raw
pastoral motif—it titillates the ladies from the church.
Big chrome scissors duel an art-deco chain saw,

and spark plugs serve as curlers in a pinch.
"Just a minute, hon, while I de-grease,"
calls out Maxx. It titillates the ladies from the church

to guess what cup-jocks, shoulder pads, or falsies
are squeezed into whose oil-stained jeans and plaids.
"Just a minute, hon, while I de-grease."

Techno-sheik teens drift in at dusk for fright fads.
"That blue liquid's two-stroke, you're soaking in it,"
quips Sammi the manicurist, in oil-stained jeans and plaids.

At the Shoppe with Nexxus headshots and logging pin-ups,
Barbara—"call me Bob"—does perms and tune-ups.
That blue liquid's two-stroke; you soak in it
while they fashion a brand new Southern man: S/he's it.

My Self My Other

I want to say, "I'm straight, no really,"
but he's so beautiful, tall and willowy,
blonde and with that disappearing face
the anima dons to elude man's gaze.

We dance on a raised wooden platform
like a boxing ring unroped, perform
long waltzing turns, athletic, neat,
with the awkward grace of boys who meet

after a long harvest and first whiskey,
each the girl of the other's dream.
Who leads? I think it must be he
who sweeps us off the platform's rim

out onto air sheerer than first ice—
we push off, tentative, then glide free,
sepia shadows rippling over bottom grass,
gaiety upheld by its own fragility. . . .

Later, touring in a buggy with my wife,
I rein before a landscape still life—
a tree, a barn, a throw of boulders,
washed hues in forms complete as integers—

when a voice from the woods like a wire
drawn through cheese finds my ear,
"My face, he's cut my face to ribbons,
come see," the voice mine as a woman's.

All I've ever wanted was to sit
in the center of a wide quietness,
but whenever I draw near it,
I'm called from this world's loveliness

back to the self's intricate dramas.
My wife sits quietly. The woman of the wood
calls me to witness traumas
I've somehow caused. If I could,

I'd leave the one and save the other,
or abandon the other and be one.
Split, fixed, framed, I can do neither,
though the air's ashimmer with danceable sun.

Among the Surma of the Kormu Valley,
A *National Geographic* Photographer

Muradit, the chalky whorls of his face paint
fingered on freshly by Chinoi this morning,
whisks my arm with his warthog-bristle crop,
whispers, "You would be good for marriage"—
notwithstanding his three wives and eight children—
and offers me a bowl of milk and blood.

I imagine myself with a lip-plate, Surma blood
charging my veins, clay-and-ochre paint
scroll-working my breasts, eight children
trailing me into the millet fields each morning.
"Perhaps one day, Muradit, but would marriage
be good for *me?*" He shoos a fly with his crop.

The women wade the sorghum, harvesting the crop
whose viscid sap sweetens the staples of blood
and milk, blended to form a balanced marriage
of proteins, a marbled swirl like half-mixed paint
with a buttery, smoky, salty bite. Each morning,
they lance and tap the cattle, the male children.

This afternoon, on the Dama's granite banks, children
use my gift of a rusted *Schick* razor to crop
each other's heads in furrows. Tomorrow morning,
Nakada will wear the iron-bead skirt: "My blood
has flowed, I am a woman." Like her face paint,
it hides by display, guarding the dowry for marriage.

I bite my lip. Soon they'll pierce hers for marriage,
banking on many cattle and fat grandchildren.
But who am I to say, who have my own face paint

(though it hides more now than displays) and a meager crop
of men in the wings. A shout goes up. The men have bloodied
themselves for the donga stick-fights this morning.

Having flocked here from nearby villages all morning,
they stand with their staffs and cheer. These fierce marriages—
sport and business intertwined—train for shedding Bumi blood,
they tell me, and settle woman claims. Angular children
perch in trees to watch, flutter above the swaying crop
of staffs, cowbirds in the rushes, an image my camera will paint.

I've seen enough this morning, so stay with the small children
who stage a marriage for me, birthing an instant crop
of raggedy babies, bloodying the river with paint.

Queen Kong Storms the Kitchen
(or, Bathing the Baby in the Sink)

Primordial slime would seem your cup of tea,
the ooze of last night's supper's hollandaise,
the fetid sump of dish soap pearled with grease
that eddies in the left-hand kitchen sink,

though now you mount the counter's dais—a queen
who's set her mind to set the state aright
and, wielding the cheddar-gilded spoon, decrees
those who've made this mess must pay, and soon—

while I, too far removed to break your fall
or check the dreg-stained crystal's pending crash,
who left you just one moment in the sink,
stand adamantly posed, afraid to blink,

and, seeing Dad thus fixed, your power swells,
as in one breakneck pivot-step you plunge
back into the sink, send gouts of water down,
then rise decked-out in a lacy soapsuds gown:

a lurid hybrid betwixt a queen and beast,
whose gaze, transformed, now glowers through the steam
that lifts in wafts of equatorial breeze
above the crowns of bobbing broccoli trees,

whose lips, possessing still the knowing lilt
that flickers sometimes in my mother's smile,
now curl back and bare their teeth—all three—
and in your grip, no fey Fay Wray, just me.

To a Student Who Reads "The Second Coming" as Sexual Autobiography

Reading your essay, I find the "widening gyre"
might be Maud Gonne's; falcon and falconer,
the disaffected lovers who can't hold
the bitter-sweet anarchy of their world
after her "blood-dimmed tide" is loosed, and everywhere
illusions of lost innocence are drowned.
Lovers, you say ("the best ones like the worst"!),
are blinded by passionate intensity.

Surely, to claim a second coming's at hand
bodes well for romance; on the other hand,
it smacks of locker-room bravado, a lout
who thinks his "vast image" a *Spiritus Mundi*
rising again, unsated, for dessert,
his prowess more a lion's than average man's,
his "slow thighs" moving. Yes, that pitiless sun
might signify his coldness after it,
her indignation's reeling desert birds
as he rolls over to a stony sleep.
More than leaving her to rock the cradle
of unprotected sex, that twice he didn't last
for her to finish, you close, "cannot be borne."

The Otter and the Shark

The line paid out until the anchor set,
shivering the hull from bow to stern. I killed
the prop, and from the inlet's pitched contours
echoes dropped about us like hoops on a peg.

Before they settled, you'd stripped and leapt,
an arcing dive, the milky seams from strap
and swimsuit bottom striping your descent.
The opal waters closed. . . .

I'd heard that nursing Grays and Makos haunt
the coves off Ku-ring-gai that time of year.
You surfaced meters out, your blunt head matted,
smug in your sleekness, rolled and dove again,

but where the gum-treed ridges sheared to water
and limestone plunged beyond sure sight, a warp
of shadow flexed toward light, tunneling deeper.
You rose, at last, retorted with a grin,

then whipped your length to rifle 'round the keel,
spurning the ladder lowered out of fear.
Tonight, again, I clutched the lifeline first,
Then saw your black fur stream, your belly flash.

Living Right

Where I come from, what they call "living right"
most often means no liquor and no sex,
except what's sanctioned by the state of marriage,
and only then with hurried indifference,
plus regular appearances at church.

Only men need worry about living right,
since women had gotten themselves, or been stuck,
minding the store of moral goods and notions
and, as far as men could tell, forgotten how
to live wrong. And so, naturally, such men,

resenting women for the only power
they'd given them to exercise, and guilty
for their aversion to living right, wrested
a counter definition from the margins
of socially acceptable behavior,

according to which they failed to love the children
the women had, in their minds, forced upon them,
and took to the woods, where they might exercise
a purgative prerogative to kill,
followed by heavy drinking, during which—

and usually while pissing side-by-side,
gazing up at a bleary moon together—
they'd in an epiphanic gush concur
that *this* was—"goddamn right!"—living right.
So, this morning when our houseguest said,

"You folks sure know how to live right," I paused.
Surely not the Southern brimstone version,
and not its sexist doppelganger either.

Not the living right that characters
in films affect—and their actors imitate—

of smoking fifty-buck cigars, driving
sports cars faster than the speed of self-inflation
until the cancer or the smash-up gets them.
And, not the New Age fix of cheating death
via a regiment of yoga classes

and fat-free, chem-free, taste-free reinforcements,
though, true, we'd served him farmer's-market fare
stir-fried in ginger sauce the night before.
If what he meant was wine for taste, laughter
spilling in waves around a room of friends,

stories that each retelling deepens, and sex
if less often then less hurried, if more
honest then hotter for it, if sometimes playful
then sometimes reverential for close enough
to church, and if, as I'd expect, all this

regulated by love of work that's good,
midway between the Buddhist Middle Way
and middle-class protesting conformity,
then, hell, let's puff a fifty-cent cigar
and go for a spin in the station wagon, honey.

Making War

And night still lingered underneath the eaves.
In the dark houseboats families were stirring
And Chinese soup was cooked on charcoal stoves.
Then one by one there came into the clearing
Mothers and daughters bowed beneath their sheaves.
The silent children gathered round me staring
And the shy soldiers setting out for battle
Asked for a cigarette and laughed a little.

—James Fenton, "In a Notebook"

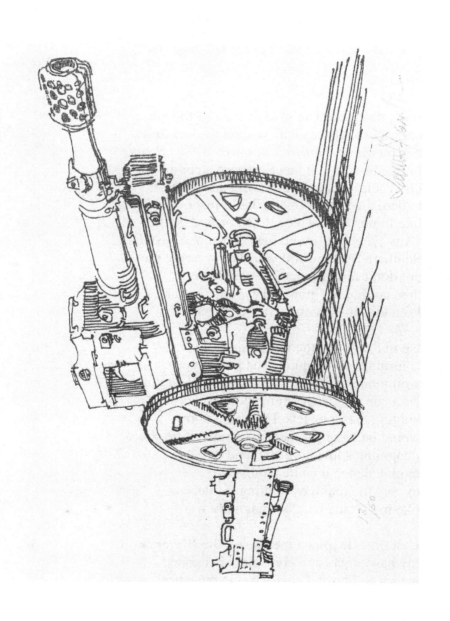

Huck Finn at Forty-One

He said it was the best fun he ever had in his life, and the most intellectural;
and said if he only could see his way to it we would keep it up all the rest of
our lives and leave Jim to our children to get out.

—Huck about Tom

Jim's dead, and I'm glad of it too, I thought
before I caught myself, reading the headlines
this morning: *Confederates fire on Fort Sumter!*
I remembered Colonel Sherburn steppin' out
his second-story window with a shotgun
to dare the town's finest, that'd just been raging
like Injuns for his hide, to come and get it.
"Any lynching 'round here'll be done past dark,
Southern fashion, and you'll be wearing masks,
but don't forget to fetch a *man* along,"
then cocked his gun, and everybody ran.
I ran too, still having a boy's excuse.

Up in St. Louis, the recruiting office
is turning ink to blood. The line wraps clean
around the building, shoulders weighed down
with papa's squirrel gun, and marbles still
bulging their pockets. I allow as Tom
would be amongst them even now, if he could,
imagining some holy war, and him
mounted atop a white Arabian
to save the realm by smiting infidels. . .
like me. Some wholly imaginary war.

Last time he joined me aboard the *Walter Scott,*
my passengers and crew already bedded,
we sat and puffed cigars inside the wheel house
and listened to the paddle splashing echoes
off the cliffs along the Missouri side.

42

Near choked ourselves to death, remembering
how Jim told us the moon had spawned the stars
and I believed him, having seen a frog
lay near as many, when the larboard chimney
belched up a flume of sparks in a spiraling eddy
that hung above the water to stern, then fell
as if the Milky Way's river of stars
had dropped down hissing into its own reflection.

That was six months past, and Tom so busy
he only rides for lawyerin' business now,
downstream to Cape Girardeau, sometimes Cairo.
It's *The Law* that Tom imagines now
will be his white Arabian, but that's
no change, so far as I reckon, for him
who rallied us to ambush oil-rich A-rabs
only to have a Sunday picnic marm
out-duel the pack of us with a bumbershoot.

About like using spoons to dig out Jim,
and picks and shovels right there in the shed.
It had to be done by the book, Tom said,
"Done *right,*" as if Jim lay in a dungeon in France
and weren't no honor in it if the digging
took us less than thirty-seven years.
The difference is, he wouldn't have gone through with it
unless *he knew* that Jim was freed already,
not even for a bullet in the leg.
The book has changed, the fable's still the same.

On moonless nights, I slow at certain bends
and watch for signals from the eastern bank.

I can make a dozen disappear
down in the hold among the bags, or topside
between the cotton bales. But that'll end
soon as the Rebels start blockades and boardings,
as will the Southern share of paying business.
Other nights, off watch, I close my eyes
and feel black water sliding 'neath my shoulders
and of a sudden raise my head to check
the cabin furniture, expecting it
to move on past like a snag. I'm on the raft.

I had that dream again last night, the one
where I'm down underneath the water and hear
the cannon's muffled boom and see the smoke
blooming slow and quiet above the river.
The voices of Judge Thatcher and my Pap
come driftin' as if whispered through a tube,
"Awful, awful, all that blood, all that. . . ."
and then the faces, pale and wavy, loom
over the railing, Tom and Aunt Polly's,
looking straight down through me. Then I hear
the distant wheebling of a sick melodeon
and some girl's voice reciting a soppy ode,
but when I reach to roll the limp corpse over
the face is not Buck Grangerford's, but mine,
the blood spreading from bullet holes is mine.

That night I woke the doc to tend Tom's leg
he asked me how a fella manages
to shoot hisself in the middle of the night,
and quicker than I should've I blurted out,

"He had a dream and it shot him." And now
twenty-seven years have flowed on past
as if we all were stuck inside that dream,
and I'm not sure if even another ten
will be enough to get Jim dug out *right*.

"Honk for Peace"

*Their monument sticks like a fishbone
in the city's throat.*
—Robert Lowell, "For the Union Dead"

The stately capital's gold-plated dome
looms severely against an El Greco sky,
and, hanging from its marble entablature,
a flag big enough to drape a dozen caskets

lolls in a groundswell. Marble steps crescendo
down the slope to a leveled terrace where,
in a fountain gushing red geraniums,
a bronze soldier readies himself for battle

perpetually: the fishbone of a memory
of wars now distant, just, and cleanly ending.
It is he whom they have come to petition,
these protesters lining the curb with posters.

Each stoplight sends a stream of faces peering
as from within TVs. Blank gazes flicker
one way or the other: a bird is flipped
from a fuming SUV, one cell-phoned mother

with kids strapped in *beep beeps,* a business man
flashes a "V"—for "victory" or "peace"?—
and a beat-up Chevy packed with tattooed teens
blares and screams the length of the block, "Hell, yeah!"

Then the local newshound vans up on the curb,
"Live at Five" with the media-poll outliers.
It is he whom they have come to petition,
though GE owns his network. Standing vigil,

they brave the cold and chant, watch for the few
who in an instant's startled recognition
witness their own unsayable deep wish
and shoot quick smiles. The soldier cannot smile

nor weep, his gaze trained beyond reflection,
though he too stands his vigil for this city
where taillights ghost red tracers in the dark
and overhead the stars are bursting in air.

War Porno

Bursts of fire pin him to a chalky column—
"Where the hell is backup!"—he drops and rolls,
spraying a clip of sparks from the nozzle
of his SAW, springs up quicker than "Salaam"

and slams on the modular grenade launcher,
when a flash from the roof drops him to one knee,
and in his mind's slow-motion camera he sees
himself pirouetting down, squeezing the trigger,

the tiny globe of fire like Tinkerbell on acid
snaking across the courtyard, lifting the man
into a spray of crimson pixels. "YOU WIN!
PLAY AGAIN?" But his dad calls, "Hey, G. I. Kid,

come take a look at *this*. Check out *these* graphics."
On Fox, digitally enhanced satellite footage
of biblical geography sweeps into softcore coverage
of faceless collateral damage, then a soldier ecstatic

for the week's first shower, his stateside parents—
"God bless!"—then back to the cannon's-eye perspective
that keeps us rubbernecking for the next live
death, the real-time bullets, the correspondent's

staticky play-by-play, then "over to you at the Pentagon."
Hard to resist, this combo of lethal and techno-glitz.
"So real, it's unbelievable." With remotes and joysticks,
armchair patriots are winning our wars. Play again?

You Talkin' to Me, Pilgrim?

"You Bin Ladin? We been loadin'!"
still boasts the poster in the window
of the *Hammer & Saw Hardware & Paint*
in Fairplay, Colorado.

The Victorian courthouse, a library now,
has seen some hombres swing.
The town's gussied up, the main drag bannered,
for the "Burrow Days" shindig.

The packin' cowboy manning the counter
leads me down the aisle for caulk
while the TV above the register flickers
Fort Apache, starring The Duke:

"A picnic, lieutenant, a picnic?" he drawls
to refugees of the New Age
who pack the chocolate boutique next door
in the name of mountain-man heritage.

But then the round-headed South Park kids
pop in for demolition supplies.
In a blink one ducks back of the counter
to swipe the cowboy's prize:

a photo, gilt-framed, of an American eagle
with a Dirty Harry squint
extends one scaly middle talon
and sneers, "Jihad this!"

Then Yosemite Sam steps around the nail bin
brandishing both his side irons.
"Reach for the sky you claim-jumpin' varmints!
One twitch and I'll be a firin'!"

Now the South Park kids are roped onto burros
headed up Breakneck Pass.
Waving his hat to the tourists, Sam winks,
"The way down's a tad treacherous."

Dun Aengus

Dun Aengus demands invaders and pilgrims
approach through outer rings, work in.
First is the sea ringing Inish Mór,
the thin, leeward band of North Atlantic
we ferried across, chewing knuckles
of gingerroot to keep our stomachs.

Some of us stood the upper deck,
legs braced, foul-weather suited,
astonished each time the bow's plunge
sent a shotgun blast of spray
into our faces, less brave by half
than those dry as dice in a box below.

Another's the ring of velvet-grassed paddocks,
the rumpled island scalped of trees
by millennia of smoked mutton, rafters
blacked by twig fires, until nothing's left
but peat and the gnarled blackthorns,
shriven harps bent by unceasing westerlies.

And, too, the walls' crazed patterns,
less to keep in sheep than clear space
to graze, leave droppings, make soil
for grass to surge once more, tenuous
purchase surviving makes on the future.
And to make the one surplus a blessing.

Then comes the ring of razored stones,
jagged headstones planted askew
with no room for the dying to lie down.

We, like them, marched up the bare mountain,
shale-backed and purplish against blue sky,
but heard no hoarse command to dash

our shins on stones offering no cover
and set in arrow range. But then,
we came as pilgrims on rented bikes
wobbling down hedge-banked lanes,
stopping at the one wayside hostel
to lunch on barley soup and salmon,

grateful to be four thousand years late.
And so weaved the razored stones
quietly, bowed through doors slotted
in the outer walls (concentric, man-tall,
leveled ground between for fighting),
and came finally to the broken crown

of Dun Aengus. Only then, having been
allowed entry, having passed through
into the central tumbler of the colossal lock
that hangs on the west-most door of Ireland,
did we see the wall's sweep round cut off
by sky where the cliff-face sheers to the sea.

Only then did we know this a cup
to catch the sun's evening sacrament.
Strangers come to a shared intimacy,
nearly stripped of the need for it,
we dropped our knapsacks and cameras to form
the inner ring that then we knew

we'd come there to join. But only after
crawling to hang our heads over the edge,
filling the windsocks of our bodies:
wind honed on a whole, slatey ocean
met the blunt edge of a continent
and rushed upward to widen rubbery faces.

Only bellies pressed to rock
convinced that we were not falling, though
the very stone beneath us hummed.
Waves came with the ease of liquid
rocked in a bowl, climbed the storied
ledges toward us, and bloomed in slow,

feathering explosions, collapsing back
only to detonate again against
incoming crests, curdling the ocean.
Gannets teetered on the wind's edge.
Puffins shot in and out of crags.
A cadmium lichen scaled the rocks.

We grew smaller than any of these,
lined along the edge, bodies already
emptied, waiting to be blessed into the sea.

Homing

And though of houses left in the past,
behind, some wink out their windows,
others reflect the leveling sun and

prong their shine into the unknown,
blindly lighted, traveling with us.
Our headlights carve the coming dark.

—James Applewhite, "Driving from Columbia"

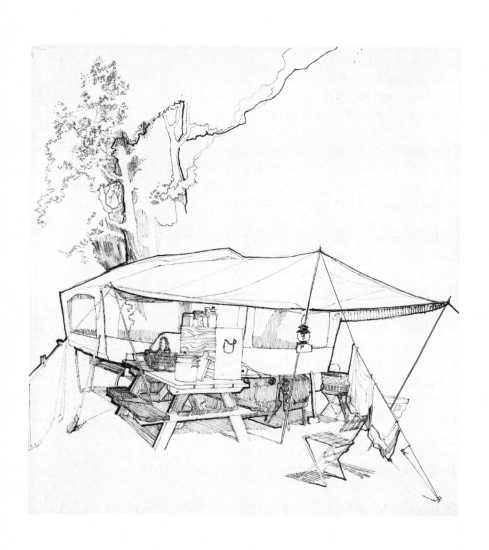

Awake

At dawn's window, the Virginia creeper,
its long summer of stretching to block the sun,
now hangs on the screen on that moment
when green goes to translucent saffron,

then, struck in the sun's embrace, infuses,
each cell seemingly lit from within, a choir
of red paper lanterns at twilight, quavering
to one muted key of unmatched desire.

Earlier, the wind shook down a few stray drops
like a child's hand slapping the roof above
our faces, but I was somewhere else. . . .
The old density of unhealed love

inhabiting that landscape, atmospheric.
The house, a listing gingerbread Victorian
with candled windows winking through hemlocks,
rickety jambs, and vision-warping panes—

a home for last-legs gentry in a Chekov play—
and weather to match, frighteningly bitter,
the coal fire blue-tonguing the grate,
the fiercely quivering red coils of heaters

no match for air shot through with the black floss
of icy breezes. And yet, a manic festivity,
a roasting aroma from the kitchen, glasses
clinking, a card game in a farther room, the levity

of uncles, the laughter of children under the stairs,
ending in cloistral bedrooms, mountainous *plumeaux,*
and hand-wound clocks whose shattering ticks
portend avalanche, blanketing snows. . . .

Did I, or did I not, choose to wake here,
still who I was then but seven times different,
and is not this a making from what's given,
the self dying and reborn in every instant?

Dungeness

One who had roots in that earlier era was Rogers Alberty. Son of a slave, he was hired as the gateboy for Dungeness at the age of five. Dressed in bottle-green livery, he stood at the gate to perform his duty.
                    —photo caption, Cumberland Island Museum

The salt marsh quickens as the sun slides up.
The ferry shoulders to the pilings. Campers
and day-pass trekkers sling on packs and herd
their kids, in dayglow shades, up the boarding ramp.

We strain to hear, above the bow wave's hiss
and thrumming diesel engines, the ranger's spiel
on island habitats, the trails that worm
through scrub oak groves to dunes and sea-oat meadows,
or south to Dungeness, the fire-charred ruins
the Carnegies bequeathed for us to mourn.
There, feral horses graze the feral lawns
on which the 'twenties high society danced
to orchestras imported from New York.

Just off the landing, the single-room museum—
an ice house once—whose foot-thick walls were poured
of a pearly sawdust and coquina batter.
Our voices automatically drop
to match the cool, sepulchral atmosphere
of history preserved in backlit blocks
of plexiglass display: the artifacts
of Indian, Conquistador, and run-
off slave arranged to trace a progress toward
lawn tennis in a jungle Xanadu,
pale arabesques of granite mounting up
like dripped sandcastle spires above the manes
of palms, the insect nation's savage gossip.

It all ends here with us, who only spectate,
who squint our way back out into the sun,
and, when an armadillo—modest accountant
of palmetto scrub—draws our stick-wielding boys
into the sepia realm of shade beneath
the canopy of myrtle oaks, we follow.
The lacework weave and sift of light betrays,
beneath each leaf, a fiercer machination.

The windward boardwalk ladders into the sun.
Desiccated pilings rise where the sand
has ebbed, sink where the sand has flooded, spilling
finely as sugar through gap-toothed planks that spill us
onto the strand. But if you pause mid-way,
jump the railing, ignore Park Service signs,
you may find a world becalmed among the dunes:
cricket tracks stitching the sand for days,
a doorless shack half filled by a blizzard's drift,
and the single wing and pitted engine block,
its pistons seized on a moment decades past. . . .

The day is gone, the ferry almost missed.
We hadn't noticed, heading out this morning,
the paper mill in the mouth of the St. Mary's,
its boiling stacks' white pennants heralding
the nuclear sub base just upstream, nor seen
the abandoned canneries that line the quay.

Shedding sandy clothes for the bath, I see,
among the ruined wine-cellar catacombs,
their tub, its claw feet reared, bouqueted with loops
of rust-gnawed pipes that could not hold it up
once fire had licked the third-floor joists away.

And there, the crumbling bookend gates where once
Rogers Alberty stood in bottle green,
who in that photo, serving drinks, was sixty.

Kosciusko, Mississippi

Mornings we gather on the verandah in rockers
to catch the winter sun's slant through the columns.
Draped in her wheelchair, Miss Ginny rocks a little
out of habit, watches the passersby and, in distant
pantomime, raises a hand to each hand that raises.

Afternoons, we climb the narrow stairs with books.
Here, in a miniature brass chest like a pirate's,
an American Legion lapel pin, a brass asterisk
with enameled insignia your granddad wore after
the Great War, and with it a pair of flashy earrings

dared once, perhaps, on a hot cotillion night—
now cracked glass and tarnish. Befuddled from naps,
we rise to voices in the hall and an amber light
ebbing from the windows; its currents threaten
to preserve us forever among the whispery murmurs.

But it's the TV blaring downstairs. Propped before it,
she is dying, she who outlived him by twenty years,
the last of six generations in this house, is dying.
Still good for a rubber of bridge, she hasn't quit.
Her good eye flashes yet with impish rage.

We could imagine your great-great-granddad
striding the main hall in riding boots with a whip,
but he was a banker and wore fine calfskin slippers.
History preaches romance, practices economics.
How can we, and how can we not,

close it behind us with the click of a brass box.

Lawrence from New Mexico, 27 October, 1922

. . .something Lawrence wrote about
in such a manner
as to make us seem magnificent.
    —Tony Hoagland, "Lawrence"

It persists in seeming like a stage to me
and not a proper world, a comic opera,
but played with solemnest intensity
by bone-rattle and tom-tom orchestra.
The Indians wrap themselves in cotton sheets
like Hamlet's father's ghost, with a lurking smile.
Walking the dung-and-dust caked Taos streets,
I feel myself. Got-up cowboy style,
Hamlet's turgid angst has lost its impetus.
I write as bread bakes in the horno oven.
A squirrel runs up the balsam pine to scold us.
Today I'll mend the pole corral, and then
Madame and I will chink the cracks with mud—
the nights already cold, fire in our blood.

Each evening, after tea, we ride Azul
and Poppy down the trail to Del Monte Ranch
to pick up mail and play a game of "pool,"
stopping to fill the skins at Lobo Branch.
We drove last week in a motor-car to see
Fort Apache Reserve. We came at sunset,
the shallow upland smoked with scattered teepees,
and horsemen crossed the dusk in silhouette
from tent to tent. Blanketed figures crouched
where naked boys threw bones at whip-tailed dogs.
The din of yelps and drums and goat bells roused
a dreadful coughing fit. Madame sat agog.
Then Tony, who was driving, turned and said,
"He not write this, that Cooper book you read?"

The City That Chooses You
(Sydney, Australia)

Hurtling north, skirting sheer coastal vistas
through stands of pom-pom-headed eucalypts
that intimate the lost prehistories
while giving way to red-tile roofs, low strips
of panel beaters, bottle shops, car lots
with red and yellow pennants snapping, then
green strips of bowling clubs, white suits and hats
arresting time, ball poised beneath a chin,

just as the road slingshots 'round Botany Bay:
here, the cloudless sky's inquisitive,
metallic water sullenly responsive,
glazed mud, fish shack, a concrete bridge, the day
an invitation awaiting your reply,
expectancy that soon you will arrive—
where?—a place suddenly you know you live,
seeing it first time with a resident's eye,

and then the other cities rise before you:
the skylines, bridges etched at dusk, and fountains
lit with colors, roundabouts, and views
of back lots, under passes, cut-through lanes
that only those who live there know. The shock
of recognition of the strange transmutes
strangeness back to houses on your block.
It dawns that life has been one long commute

from almost home to not yet home. But now,
this place begins to feel like yours, this city
that throws its arms around an ocean, plows
the Opera House's savage civility

into rocks breaking with light, fireworks
making the bridge's fretwork shadows dance,
or a yacht regatta carving the blue expanse
while tour-boat guides give local legends a torque,

loudspeakers echoing from the mansioned shores.
But these are only the staged culmination.
Before them, Grande Parade's beach-kitsch stores,
the fish-and-chips, the Lotto stands, and soon
the 1940s bathing-house gazebo
and beach signs showing a dog bit like a cookie.
Then Oxford Street's Turkish-bizarre row
where Oliver Twist and Kim play hooky.

Even the platform-shoed and pock-faced girls
at King's Cross; even the Road Department blokes,
three leaning on their shovels, takin' a smoke-o,
to guarantee this jam's horn-blaring swirl;
even the sharks that window shop the harbor's
steel-netted beaches, chomping to have a go
at human sashimi, are yours, all yours,
at this one moment in the rending flow.

The Road to Canberra, and Beyond

Jumbucks graze on Lake George today, white puffs
from distant artillery, or thought balloons
emptied of words, blown toward the sear horizon.
What water there may be sulks in the sloughs

beneath the crust of sod and reckless grasses,
but mostly waits in clouds a decade away.
And here, a geologic shrug has tilted gravity,
combing the trees off-plumb. This side of Yass,

the *Big Merino* straddles the petrol pumps,
its giant crook'd horn a cornucopia
for proud convict descendants turned bourgeois.
Ned Kelly's ghost, visored and gauntleted, gallops

alongside our *Ford,* which has made a platypus
of *Holden*—robbery masked as politics.
The Aboriginal "breast" in Canberra's fixed
with Parliament Building's giant white octopus. . . .

This quirky, sly, soft-spoken, mother country's
nonplussed by Commonwealth or fatherland.
The wind-lathed, luminous continent stands
beyond the Black Stump, on past Gundagai,

while most shout rounds in bowling clubs in Sydney.
Out here, where few will see, shrimp-pink galahs
stream like tropical fish—desert Priscillas—
And one day sheep will swim into the sky.

The Walls of the West of Ireland

Whether because it's farthest from the east
or too rugged for a British peer's estate,
here the children still speak Gaelic first.
And, too, the walls' crazed patterns seem

to articulate something everywhere
and secret. Built less to keep in sheep than clear
space to graze, seed grass, and bury,
these walls are not the fence lines of America,

dissecting landscape regardless of its lay.
More like yarn on a rumpled counterpane,
disorder to a mind that's trained to think
Nature's what it is that humans arrange.

The order's closer up. Each rough syllable
wedged into the syntax of surface and edge,
no meaning but in context. Each segment
tells centuries of days of hands birthing

stones from sucking mud or hard-packed sod,
said along with grunts, oaths, and swapped jibes
like beads in one connective rosary. God—
half sacrament and chant, half speaking blackthorn—

let the days and voices lap together
so no one voice can rise above the rest.
Make the story wend these hills forever,
and no man force an ending. Let birds

and airborne spirits read the accidental
as intent, the irregular weave of this stone net
cast against hazard over the land,
cemented only by the untold crannies.

The Persistence of Place

Already my ghost is fading from those rooms,
these rooms, now that habit of thought's
transported me back to inhabit them once more.
Like all ghosts, I've forgotten what it is I ought

to be seeking, here in the stunned vacancy of our den,
in the perpetual dusk of nostalgia, and so find myself
lingering, peering about absentmindedly,
an unexpected guest in my own past life.

My children are living happily in another city
with me, but I miss them, orphaned as they now are
from a place of the childhood they don't yet know
was theirs. So, I drift through their rooms, a diver

revisiting spectral gangways and cabins,
or like the man who goes to work and returns
home to find everything inexplicably gone—
dents in the carpet, fill-in-the-blank dust patterns—

and can only stare with rapturous fascination
at details that never were so much themselves:
this wall's geography of rivering cracks
and continental stains, that odd wedge of shelves

beneath the stairs, these porcelain clothes hooks.
Startling, so much of us is absent, absence.
I sometimes think we *are* the places we've lived,
less that we leave behind some part of us

than that each leaves in us a part of it,
becoming the map that guides as we fill it in.
Like all ghosts, I go on hungering to settle
with myself, but I'm not home. Yet. Again.

Totem Animals

I am hearing the shape of the rain
Take the shape of the tent and believe it,
Laying down all around where I lie
A profound, unspeakable law.
I obey, and am free falling slowly

Through the thought-out leaves of the wood
Into the minds of animals.

—James Dickey, "In the Mountain Tent"

Porc d'Espine

He made a certain squalor in the moonlight of the Rocky Mountains.
—D. H. Lawrence, "Reflections on the Death of a Porcupine"

At four o'clock
in the mountain's mineral dark
something nameless comes to knock.

It seems to gnaw
the log my snoring saws
in a rhythm steady and without pause

like long-abiding
and dogged lovers testing,
in some adjacent room, the springs.

I sink into the embrace
of dream, then bolt up, braced.
No one but me in this wintry place,

no phone, no gun,
the floor joists of the cabin
shivering: a fitting visitation

for a moonless night,
darkness thick as graphite,
the air suddenly quick with spirits.

What are you?
The hungry ghost of a Sioux
in war headdress? Wood or glue—

what's your craving,
crouched with head working
like a self-fed machine set lathing?

No animal I've seen,
more like a child's drawing,
a sea urchin crossed with a soup tureen,

but a pine-knot knobkerrie
hurled from the porch's safety
sends you off, though in no hurry.

You pig misbegot,
you stubby little inkpot,
you miniature bull bristling bandarillas,

I know who you are,
your nibs dipped in cinnabar,
each tethered by its glint to a star.

Further Reflections on the Death of a Porcupine

*I've been seedy, and I've grown a real beard, behind which I shall take
as much haven henceforth as I can, like a creature under a bush.*
                                        —D. H. Lawrence

Lawrence, in Taos
you admired the square-eyed pueblos,
stacked like boxes above the arroyos,

and the Sangre de Cristo range,
banked above the desert's mirage
of deep-sea bottom, a cloud's anchorage.

At the adobe rancho,
far removed from Gudrun's chateau,
you put on Eden and named it "Lobo"

after yourself.
Apaches loined with fox pelts
tamped the earth with flat feet and yelped,

*Yo way yo hi ya,
Yo way yo hey ya. . .hey ya,*
and the smoke bore totem animacula

into your head. You said,
"Old demon, I have been spirited.
Touch me carefully, father, my beard is red."

Having relinquished
speed, cunning, and keenness
of senses, he came to you as witness

of other skills:
not first the magazine of quills,
but a certain willingness to be still

in the face of violence,
long memory and steady balance,
a sufficiency to solitude and catholic palate.

It was not for Miriam,
the black-eyed cow, alarmed
at milking time, nor for Madame,

who shivered her refusal
at the dog's return, puzzled
by the "awful beard" dangling from its muzzle,

nor for simple hate
of his lumbering beetle's gait,
his "pallid, living bush which swayed,"

that you shot him.
Not even for the "fourth dimension"
of your vitalistic, Darwinian Buddhism.

"A subtle dragon stings us
in the midst of plenty. *Quos
vult perdere Deus, dementat prius.*"

Those whom God wished
To damn, he first drove mad.
Not wolf, but a subtler self you refused.

Mouse Poem for La Petite

He was a cheeky fellow, you bet,
crossing our floor, and in no hurry,
pausing to groom his whiskers, set
his cowlick up with one brusque paw,
throw us a glance like Peter Lorre,
too bored to be malevolent,
as we three watched with slackened jaws.

"Go get him, La Petite!" I said,
"Aren't you a self-respecting cat?"
And, taking umbrage, down she poured,
as if to say, "Oh, don't you worry,"
demur as a scheming diplomat,
and padded across the hardwood floor.
We turned once more to love's inquiry.

Waked with a start, I see La Petite
standing by, sphinx-like, attendant,
too self-impressed—bemused? discrete?—
to walk across my face and gore
the half-mauled little smarty pants
she's dropped upon my balance sheet.
Is that, I see, a raised whisker?

But more the butt in this than I,
he's frozen like a cartoon convict
palsied in the spotlight's eye,
and in that beat I half expect

he'll break into a tap-dance shtick,
stammer a Woody Allen alibi,
but he's got plans I don't suspect,

and makes a dash beneath the spread,
headed down toward—Holy Shit!
What do you do with a rodent cupped
between the sheet and your softest skin?
"He'll gnaw to freedom through my gut"—
the thought that flashes through my head,
one moment's pause to count my sins.

La Petite, my slit-eyed bishop,
I absolve myself through him.
I'll not turn Judas, give him up
for thoroughly devoted torture,
nor toss him in the toilet's maelstrom,
but full pardon is where I stop
(am I confessing or confessor?).

Knowing his ways inveterate,
knowing his boater, cane, and spats
would tap again across my plate,
and, having firsthand experience
at dancing for one's supper, I scat
to the posh townhouse's parking lot,
and shoo him toward our inheritance.

Squirrelly

Fattened on bushels of birdseed they've stolen,
these are the squirrels one might see in *Denny's*
taking up half of a booth, walrus-shouldered as

sons of Nebraska who toss about hay bales or
bankers who squat on their nut-hoards of zeros.
Still, how they ready their haunches so daintily,

shifting their weight like prissy stenographers,
launching themselves then to the "Squirrel-Proof Feeder"—
now there is an oxymoronic expression—and

nimbly trapeze it with the greatest of ease.
When a single claw latched in a nick proves sufficient to
traverse the vertical face of Mount Everest,

it's I who am dangling twixt *bastard* and *'at-a-boy,*
and when the feeder's slick roof sets one skittering
off of the edge for some antic back-peddling

it's I who am flailing in laughter's suspension.
Who is more squirrelly, I ask you, the squirrel or
the man who sits squinting at squirrels with fury,

cobbles together from duct-tape and chicken wire
baffles of which only he is the victim,
the Elmer Fudd gawking with baffled befuddlement?

In what proportions are mixed the tenacity,
numb-skulled myopia, sportive abandon,
to keep at the tough nut, despite all past failures and

promised rejections? Out walking, I watch a pair
catapult, scamper-dance, amorously wrestling, then
skedaddle back home to zip on this squirrel suit.

Chocolate and the Manatees

Triton astride the dolphins, he stands in the stern
of his twin-outboard launch, braced legs tanned
to the color of his name, and grips a throttle
in each back-thrust hand as we churn

from the dock, then plane toward the windward cayes.
We clutch our new hats and squint. He beams
like Teddy Roosevelt—all bully teeth and mustache—
or like Hemingway's Old Man who sees

the sweet line of promise slicing his palm.
Now, he polls in a hush, watches for shadows to lift
from the kelp forest's canopy like dirigibles.
"There she is, yes, oh, you are lovely, my darling"—his psalm

as tender as any sailor's to a mermaid—
"Oh, you beautiful girl, yes, come to me."
And she does: bristled elephant-hide nostrils
snuffle the surface, eyes more curious than afraid

blink us into focus. A shushing cannonade of shutters.
The woman of the couple from Hamburg blurts, *"Schwein,"*
and I hope his third language isn't German, he
who chicken-wings his elbows to show her flippers

plucking a ganglia of roots from the sea bed
with the delicate white scallops of her nails. "Look!"
he hisses, "A bull pursues her, see!" But I,
having crossed my legs an hour now, must thread

sternward through the standing company of voyeurs,
who avert their gaze as, isometrically
between the engine and the gunwale—"See, he chases her
until she catches him"—I lower into the rapture

of release, the enveloping water cool and delicious. . . .
A pair of leathery soft arms pulls me deeper,
she breathes into me the amplitude of her love,
Ignore those arid lovers, they only envy us.

Apologia to the Opossums

I. Tennessee

Caught in the open, what else could they do
but scurry faster down the fallow cornrows
on Williams Island? And what else but pursue,
the pack of us flapping and cawing like crows?

Jesus, they were ugly as day-old dishwater,
snouts lined with yellow needles, capped at the end
with a pink button like a pig's. What doubts
their ancient, nutmeat brains could apprehend

came true when we snatched them up by the tails,
tails segmented and mottled pink as worms.
They hissed like cobras, curled up like snails,
quivering to sink those teeth into our arms,

but a knuckled thump on the skull made the possum
play possum, bow to the big thing that had them.
For us, a hijinks, no heroic triumph,
but when the river canyon's wind caromed

across the fields of ruffled grass heads toward us,
we held them up as trophies. It was then,
with finely fingered hands folded and loose,
their eyes pressed closed as if just stopped to listen,

they offered what it was we had to learn.
Some we freed, some paddled over the fish beds
to Ella V, who gorged them a week on sweet corn
to purge the taste of garbage and fish heads.

"A cross 'tween pork and dark-meat chicken," she said.

II. Australia

Waking dry mouthed, certain I'd heard it again
jiggling the door latch, entering, sure I glimpsed
a shaping darkness in the hall like the fin
of a Great White carving lightless waters, convinced

by weeks of nightly visitations that some demon
pursued me, whether of my own fabrication
or sprung through the portal from an otherworldly zone,
I could no longer tell, holding my breath to listen.

Then Adrian, the *Qantas* pilot next door, mentioned
possums in his attic. . . ."Yeah," I said, "I guess
that's common here," and slunk away relieved and chastened,
no kangaroos in my top paddock, just a pest.

That night again I heard the dry bones rattled, tried
to tell myself, "It's just a critter in the garret."
Peering up, I peered down where the plumbers pried
the floorboards from my childhood house's toilet:

There, the thirty-seven skeletons, the skulls
grinning in repose, the paisley curls of vertebrae
perfectly preserved. We were the infidels,
and now their curse had tracked me, half a world away.

III. Florida

Vast sanctuary of marsupials,
Australia must have granted them to us.
How else explain the leak in that gene pool:
the slope-shouldered, discreet, and dubious

cousin that rattles backyard bins and gives
my farmer neighbor's roaming bitch a run?
Could a band of half-drowned monsoon refugees
have rafted a downed tree across an ocean,

making landfall in Chile before the tradeoff
between their foodstuff and flotation sunk them?
And why'd we get the one so hard to love?
What evolutionary prank or whim

would change the soft-furred, perky ones that leaped
from eucalypts to board our deck Downunder
and sit on their haunches with suppliant hands,
for our rat-tailed slouchers? As Randy Newman said,
"He may be a fool but he's our fool"—a reminder
of the vain love that being us demands.

IV. North Carolina

You, little ghost, whom the Algonquin
in the Monongahela Valley called

apasum, "white animal," revenant
of twilight and of dawn, you

84

who know scavenging is purest
economy, who would not shun

a small offering or allow the self
importance of others to rob you

of the private pleasures, you who even
in your reticence speak directly

to death and know better than we
the vanity of fearing the unseen—

forgive us, forgive us who fail
to carry our children on our backs,

who forget what we know early
of climbing to safety, who hate

the pigeon, the carp, and the rat
for being neither wholly wild

nor fully tame, hating our own
in-between state. You, Old Mother,

come to me now, lead me out past
the canting sheds, across the fields,

and into the recesses of the healing wood.

Full Emptiness

A self inside self, cool as conscience, one to be erased
in your final night, or faxed, still knows beneath
all the mute grand opera and uncaused effect—
that death which can be imagined is not true death.
—Les Murray, "Corniche"

Where We Lay Down

We slept that summer on the second-story porch,
our cots within arm's reach, and talked of school
or a trick played on Charlotte. Our voices dropped
as the watery half-light drew itself back out
through the cut-paper layerings of leaves.

When the chorus of trees began to whine and pitch,
the leaves singing the song of distances,
and someone took the sky and shook it out
with sparks like mother shook from white laundry,
the rain beat through the screen, and we leapt up,

scooting the cots to the center of the floor, jumped back
in the damp sheets, shivering though it was hot.
The next flash fixed us in a marble frieze.
Years later, waking in the receding tug of dream,
you'll hear again the runoff falling from the eaves

in rivulets, drops, then slower, heavier drops,
and find the line of pock marks in the dirt,
and lift your head to see the slice of roof
against the sky's blue invitation, which you
accepted, and know that Charlotte is dead

and so somehow still too young to join us
in the darkening air. Recall for me then what
I always meant to say before it began
when the leaves drop and turn at once in a hush:
if this storm will take me, I will give it my arms and rise up.

The Leggers

Strapped onto planks ahead of the boat lie men
suspended on their backs above the water

and walking with their legs against the walls.
Their shadows stride vastly before the lanterns.

The roof drips. They spider forward, pass
an open shaft beneath which faint dusk stands

upon the water. My face is not my own.
Upstream, a past I don't yet know is mine:

the tunnel opening's daylight disc a coin
flickering from the bottom of a well,

a wish like the small end of a telescope.
And when the leggers in their terrible striding

begin to sing, their voices loom in a vibrant,
blurry booming along the moss-furred walls:

Each now's twice doubled by a then—
One leads on to the next event,
One casts a light back where we've been.
The way we go is the way we went.
The way we go's the way we went. . . .

In Search of the Lost Indian Princess

The alligator, who has five distinct calls:
friendliness, love, mating, war, and a warning—
whimpers and speaks in the throat
* of the Indian Princess.*
                    —Elizabeth Bishop, "Florida"

As the sun goes down
on the sput-sput of lawn sprinklers
in St. Pete, the long shush
and dull clink of shuffleboard ceases.

The mammoth white-stucco hotels
begin to glow in the dusk
with a kind of vacant dignity.
I can feel foundations settling

those critical inches toward sea level,
windowsills crumbling, moist
and soft as angel food cake.
Ah, the insidious leisure of decay!

I'm driving a rented car
down palm-lined boulevards.
The traffic signals bob with wind
off the bay, their Christmas colors sad

and directing no one, surely not me.
After blocks of derelict sidewalk,
faded life vests dangling askew
in murky storefronts,

I pull to a light beside
the Arthur Murray School of Dance,
the whole corner a wedge of light
sealed in plate glass.

The floor sways with gray-haired couples
holding each other with ease
and affection, turning in sure slowness
to a music I can't hear.

Suspended among lurking
and disinterested facades,
they drift in an otherworldly glow.
The light goes green.

Ahead, the road extends
into the wavering salt flat of the Bay.
The palms, stooped ancestral gods,
gently clack their manes and nod.

The *Mackinaw* Heads South

From Charlevoix Harbor we slid down Lake Michigan
past Manistee, Ludington, Muskegon, and Holland.
When her fifty-two feet of dry teak felt the pitch again,

the hull groaned like a whale on the beach at low tide
'til the gathering momentum approached fifteen knots,
which uplifted the prow to a wake-breasting glide,

her twin Chryslers gargling like rocks in a blender.
Two weeks before, cocktail ice floated these waters—
two minutes and your arms couldn't pull you up the ladder.

The console's red timing-light monitor showed
in the starboard-side engine an unhealthy flutter
of pulse, and the water compressed by the load

of the boat's own displacement beaded the planks
down below in the hold, where the deafening engines
sat crouching and shivering in a darkness that stank

of electrical shorts, while about their braced feet
two inches of oil-pimpled water step-danced,
but the bilge pump's treadling tick sounded sweet.

Just off of Grand Haven, the leaden horizon
shrink wrapped around us its nimbus of fog.
Hands clutching the wheel, Blair squinted his eyes on

the wiper blades spreading a slushy ice buildup
through which winking harbor lights dwindled to pinpricks
while bro' Henry lay snoring below. So, I suited up

in the new foul-weather gear, yellow and acrid
as asparagus piss, and then hand-over-handed
the lifeline's arc forward to peer from the bowsprit. . . .

The parting clouds showed not the ramparts of Shangri La
but a jetty of granite, twenty yards, closing fast:
"hard starboard!", I bellowed, Blair swung a parabola,

and the brass-plated strake on our beam ground the stone.
That was only the first night, when Henry slept through his death
then awoke to a sailor's night out on the town,

or as much of a night as such sailors can drown.

Germanic Traincar Constructions

Emotions, in my experience, aren't covered by single words. I don't believe in "sadness," "joy," or "regret." Maybe the best proof that the language is patriarchal is that it oversimplifies feeling. I'd like to have at my disposal complicated hybrid emotions, Germanic traincar constructions like, say, "the happiness that attends disaster." Or: "the disappointment of sleeping with one's fantasy." I'd like to show how "intimations of mortality brought on by aging family members" connects with "the hatred of mirrors that begins in middle age." I'd like to have a word for "the sadness inspired by failing restaurants" as well as for "the excitement of getting a room with a minibar."
           —Jeffrey Eugenides, *Middlesex*

I. The Happiness that Attends Disaster

In bad German that might be *das Glückaufwartendesaster,*
though this could call to mind an allegorical farce
in which Happiness, played by a beaming pigtailed miss
with twin steins, waits table upon Don Juan De Saster.

Germanic economy may suggest *das Glückimunfall*—
the happy accident—as when the dying woman's poor husband
distractedly takes a twin bag from the luggage stand
and buys her life-saving surgery with a bank robber's windfall.

A german cousin to these—*die Fröhlichkeitenkatastrophe*—
is redolent of a Gilligan's Island of frolicking mishaps
lit by a washed-up bale of Colombian weed, perhaps,
on the next wave, a case of condoms—a good-time catastrophe.

But my favorite for symmetry is *das Glückimunglück*—
the good fortune of misfortune—opposite of the gambler's card
or that silver-lining alibi for God's inexplicable disregard,
but for all lovers met through misadventure or collision, brute luck.

II. The Disappointment of Sleeping with One's Fantasy

That conspiratorial snicker and sneer
men share at the expense of women
limbered me up with this question:
"Do you know what *eternity* is?" I heard
galactic dust whistling through the aperture
of a black hole to the acetylene spasm
and depthless kiss of Heaven. I floated
there, adrift in the Big Bang's chasm.

And then, either because time sheered
or my buddy milked the smirking pause
before the punch line, I reheard the clause,
"To have and to hold from this day forward. . .
till death us do part" and shivered
at the echo of iron doors clanging fast
down an infinitely receding corridor
called *forever,* or, *as long as it lasts.*

"It's the time between when you come
and she falls asleep so you can leave."
Chuckles and nods. Nearby, my love
of decades by then—"his longest one-night stand,"
she quips—stands apart to give the men room
for sniffing crotches, she who showed me
how to slip fantasy through a wedding band
and leave disappointment for eternity.

III. Intimations of Mortality Brought on by Aging Family Members

The airplane door agape, the engines deafening,
  the warped curvature of the porthole grants
    a glimpse of Grandma disappearing
into the latté froth of a cloud's bouffant,
  laughing, and trailing wisps of her life story. . .
fallings from us, vanishings.

Father and Mother, though divorced for decades,
  share soothing thoughts borne of human suffering:
    "Life's no dress rehearsal," she sings;
"Old age ain't for sissies," with a shake of his head,
  now no one stands between them and that threshold,
queued and clipped onto the zip-line.

Brothers and sisters, we can almost ignore them,
  fumbling with our straps and swapping jibes, until
    the joke comes 'round to who goes next,
then mock courtesy of Tweedle Dee and Dum,
  then notice these are not parachutes but ballast—
intimations subtle as anvils.

IV. The Hatred of Mirrors that Begins in Middle Age

That oval by the bed—remorseless familiar—
or those sullen slabs of light in public restrooms.

You'd think we would avoid them then. But no,
we peer right in, as though we were not there,

then pull up short in startled recognition,
Is that really you, old friend? I almost didn't. . . .

Still there, that face beneath the face when you
hauled yourself up to stand in mother's room

and snagged your eyes in the glass and knew yourself,
for the first time, separate from the world.

Now every mirror tells that story again.
Like Arnold Böklin's self-portrait, the artist

a bearded man with unkempt hair who's paused
with paintbrush poised midair, his eyes fixed hard

on you who centuries later hold this place
and so can only mirror the fierce resolve

to go on painting yourself into existence.
But note the head, rotated a quarter turn,

the ruddy cusp of the right ear presented,
the left cocked back to catch the notes that fall

from a fiddle clamped beneath a skull's set grin.
The music—whether of cats in a burlap sack

struck on a curb, or of such somber beauty
all his will must be summoned not to drop

the brush and listen—we can never know.
Only he hears that tune, as we our own.

V. The Sadness Inspired by Failing Restaurants

We drive past them with the mildest interest
the way one flips past the obituaries of strangers,
the dead-eyed facades and padlocked entrances,
the bankruptcy notice—or is it an auction flier?—
like a wanted poster stuck askew on the door.

Then you recall, yes, someone had said the food
was good, but you never gave them a chance. . . .
Oh, well. Looking closer you might glimpse
the man in the crisp apron, standing spread-legged
with his arms folded across his barrel chest.

He never meant to live a Hopper painting,
the one where the edges of things are remorselessly
hard, the light from the street slices
through the lettered glass like a guillotine,
the darkness in corners dimensional with sadness.

There, the exact weight of his dream, an ash
the size of Brooklyn lodged in his chest:
the gala opening night, backstage expectancy
fanning through the kitchen, each fresh table
borne up by the flicker of a candle's beacon.

So much for romance, he thinks, balls up the apron
to toss in the mop corner, reaches to snap
off the lights, but is transfixed: not by regret,
not in self-loathing, nor even with hatred of circumstance,
which curses the gods for what we have chosen—

simple emotions he might have embraced—
but by the swelling in his chest of. . .what is it?
I think there is no word. He thinks, *happiness?*

VI. The Excitement of Getting a Room with a Minibar

If you were Gidget or Gigi or Glorianne from Kansas,
you might kick both feet up behind like a miniature pony,
sending the pleated skirt too high, squeal and run
to bounce on the bed with flipped cockroach legs.

But instead you are tired after the happy disaster, the bad
fantasy, the aging family members and mirror phobia,
not to mention the failed restaurant. This isn't Daytona
Bike Week, nor your first time in Paris, and you are

all too aware what they charge for those dinky bottles.
No, you've brought your own fifth, picked up
at *Dino's Liquor and Car Wash* before you checked in.
Today was not the day your happy childhood predicted.

You are sad with a sadness only a single room matches.
This is your reward, this view of curtained windows
exactly like yours, these industrially sanitized towels,
this generic solitude. You slip off your shoes

and click on the scrolling menu of tonight's movies:
a meteor the size of Cleveland, or sadistic murder
justifies the most thorough revenge ever quenched.
Things are looking up. You amble over to the minibar,

lift the white fluted paper cap from the cafeteria glass,
and crack your bottle of *Sky*. For just one moment,
your heart soars: there, in the plastic bucket,
still smoking with cold, perfect lozenges of ice.

Anatman

It is the emptiness-of-my-self-existence that the world is full of.
—Nolan Pliny Jacobson, *Understanding Buddhism*

From the shadows of the crib's bars cast
across the sheet, the window's day-long dialing
     of fingering light
  like a fan opening then
folding toward sleep, and the quietness in the house;

  from TV westerns and the tactics
of ambush in the Powells' ruined apple orchard,
     the hard ones that stung,
  the soft ones, skins like parchment,
rupturing their sun-warmed juices on impact;

  from notebooks overflowing homework
until it inundates dreams with unannounced
     tests, the legacy
  of standardized measuring
up, the craved *well done*'s unoffered or hard won—

  from these, came the thirst to be the person
I thought I must. This I learned from the first day's
     intensive practice.
  The farm, cloistered in hills
of sea-breeze-combed grasses, its barn spirited

  by incense spirals, candle flickers,
the susurrus of soul's interrogations,
     backed onto a creek
  we walked in meditation.
There, beneath the row of swaying poplars, grew

berry bushes so laden with fruit
their spears bowed, their clustered globes released, fell, splashed:
       this tenuous hold,
  tigers pacing below, oh,
all I wanted was one of those blackberries.

Who wants, who? The mind hungers, recoils
in a lightless room, groping for knob or switch,
       voices redoubling
  from the walls a riot of
me, me, me to drown out the guiding quiet,

  until the back, bent so long at task
that straightening might break it, unstrings its bow,
       and breath, freed, flushes
  the lungs arborations like
molten lead a die, columning up the spine,

  and a voice, neither yours nor other's,
speaks directly from the stillness of midnight
       like a waking bell
  struck: *The puddle's reflection
is not the moon, nor the thirst for self a self.*

Autumnal Equinox

Lolling on the back deck in the sun
at the moment it eases into Libra,
I feel a perfect equilibrium struck,

and though it is mid-morning, the sun,
scattering its shipwreck's coins
on the sea bottom beneath the crabapple,

shines with that dreamy quality of light
I know mid-afternoon will match precisely:
resolution balancing expectancy.

I slump into a comfortable sadness, but then,
like a teetering bamboo fountain, I tip
into joy, refilling all the while with sadness.

When the breeze lifts, the stirred leaf shadows
are mesmerist's hands. Millennia of clouds
sweep over the face of the earth, again

as before the sun keyholes the stone
to flare in the facets of chiseled hieroglyphs,
wine runnels chest hair and bared breasts

as Persephone falls to the arms of her dark lover,
and the ruddy harvest tumbles into root cellars.
I can hear the infinite host of insects

genuflect in unison around the globe,
the circadian clocks resetting in the breasts
of every goshawk, hummingbird, and peafowl.

A crabapple falls into my lap. Opposite the stem,
a puckered brown anus that was the flower.
I turn it on my palm, yellow to pink to crimson.

Notes and Dedications

"Among the Surma of the Kormu Valley": Responds to a *National Geographic* article, with stunningly beautiful photos, on the Surma of Ethiopia. With respect for the Surma people and with apologies to the photographer whose persona I borrowed as the speaker.

"Anatman": This Sanskrit word (*anatta* in Pali), sometimes translated as "no self," refers to the Buddhist doctrine according to which the concept of an essential autonomous self is an illusion that is a primary cause of human suffering.

"Apologia to the Opossums": In section III, the Randy Newman quote is from his song "Rednecks," which there refers to Lester Maddox, a greasy Southern 'possum.

"Autumnal Equinox": In particular, the one that occurred at 9:44a.m. Mountain Time, 22 September 2008.

"Chocolate and the Manatees": Set in Caye Caulker, Belize, this alludes to the mythology of the mermaid as deadly seductress, combined with reports from early European explorers who mistook manatees for mermaids. In memory of Gay Wilentz.

"The City That Chooses You": This poem owes a debt to "Here" by Philip Larkin, to whose poetry I owe much more than that.

"Dungeness": With respect for Rogers Alberty. Dedicated to Jim, Susan, Will, and Sam Watkins.

Full Emptiness: This section title is an unavoidably inadequate translation of the Buddhist concept of śūnyatā (suññatā in Pali), illuminated by *The Fundamental Wisdom of the Middle Way (Mūlamadhyamakakārikā)* by Nāgārjuna (150–250 CE).

"Further Reflections on the Death of a Porcupine": Quotes first a traditional Apache "Honoring Song" and then Lawrence's bastardized Latin, which my colleague, Dr. Nancy Ciccone, translates as, "God wants to ruin those whom first he makes crazy," perhaps love-crazy, perhaps from Ovid, Metamorphosis, 10.611–13 or 9.728-730. With respect and deference to the Apache people, and with thanks to Nancy.

"Germanic Traincar Constructions": With gratitude to Mr. Eugenides. Section II is dedicated to Judy. Section III contains two borrowings from Wordsworth and is dedicated to Barbara Lee Lucas-Dolan. Section VI is for Henry.

"Huck Finn at Forty-One": By my calculation based upon *The Adventures of Huckleberry Finn,* Huck would have been 41 in 1861 at the start of the Civil War. With a reverent bow to Dr. Martin Luther King, Jr.

"Julian Bream": Dedicated to my stepfather, Perry Virgil Lane (1921–2001).

"Kosciusko, Mississippi": Dedicated to Mabry Carnes Lucas (1901–1991), "Ginny," which was pronounced as in "guinea hen."

"Lawrence from New Mexico, 27 October, 1922": The date is fictitious and the poem not based on any specific writing of D. H. Lawrence, but he was in New Mexico in October 1922.

"The Leggers": Responds to a passage from Jill Patton Walsh's young-adult novel *A Chance Child.* Thanks to Ms. Walsh for her permission to adapt her words into verse. The song lyric, which I imagine as the chorus of a Scotch-Irish ballad transplanted to Appalachia, is original. Dedicated to Robert Donnan.

"McGaulie's Polo Grounds": The form is derived from James Fenton's "In a Notebook," one stanza of which I use as the epigraph to the "Making War" section of this book.

"The Otter and the Shark": Set at Pittwater, north of Sydney, Australia, which has no native otter. With thanks to Seamus Heaney, who does it better in "Otter." For Judy.

"Personal Effects": Dedicated to William Henry Trotter (1902–1991).

"Porc d'Espine": The title derives from an archaic French name, "pig with spines."

"Queen Kong Storms the Kitchen": For Emma Lee Smith.

"The Road to Canberra, and Beyond": In memory of Les Murray, whose every poem reinvents the English language as Australian, and better for it, and who did me the honor of publishing this poem.

"Sky": For Tyler Milne Franklin.

"Sons and Fathers": Written on Father's Day, June 20, 2004, for James Rodman Franklin (1932–2013). Marvin Gaye's father shot and killed him in 1984. Thanks to Mozart's *Don Giovanni* for the closing image.

"Squirrely": Dedicated to Margaret Bauer.

"You Talkin' to Me, Pilgrim?": John Wayne's Western characters addressed multiple others as "pilgrim." Fairplay, CO, is, or is in, South Park. For Brad Mudge and Jenny-Lynn Ellis.

"War Porno": Prompted by Joanne Ostrow, "'War porno' gives birth to new addiction," *The Denver Post,* Sunday April 6, 2003, with thanks to Ms. Ostrow. "SAW" is Squad Automatic Weapon, the M249 light machine gun.

"Where We Lay Down": Dedicated to Charlotte Llewellyn Franklin (1958–1976).

About the Author

Jeffrey Franklin grew up in Chattanooga, TN, though for over 20 years he's called Colorado home. His previous poetry collection is *For the Lost Boys* (Ghost Road Press, 2006). His poems have appeared in many literary journals, including *Crab Orchard Review, Hudson Review, Measure, New England Review, Rattle, Shenandoah, Southern Humanities Review,* and *Southern Poetry Review.* A manuscript of his received the Robert H. Winner Memorial Award from the Poetry Society of America, and his poetry has appeared in *Best American Poetry.* Since 2000 he has served as the poetry editor for the *North Carolina Literary Review,* selecting the finalists for the annual James Applewhite Poetry Prize. He received his MFA and Ph.D. from the University of Florida and works as a professor of English at the University of Colorado Denver, teaching mostly the history of the English novel and critical theory and writing. His recent scholarly books are *The Lotus and the Lion: Buddhism and the British Empire* (2008) and *Spirit Matters: Occult Beliefs, Alternative Religions, and the Crisis of Faith in Victorian Britain* (2018), both from Cornell University Press. He lives in Denver with his lifetime partner, Judy Lucas.

Made in the USA
Coppell, TX
24 November 2021

66345263R00066